Exploring Planets
URANUS

Susan Ring

WEIGL PUBLISHERS INC.

Published by Weigl Publishers Inc.
350 5th Avenue, Suite 3304, PMB 6G
New York, NY USA 10118-0069
Web site: www.weigl.com
Copyright 2004 WEIGL PUBLISHERS INC.

Library of Congress Cataloging-in-Publication Data

Ring, Susan.
  Uranus / by Susan Ring.
      v. cm. -- (Exploring planets)
Includes index.
Contents: Introducing Uranus -- What's in a name? -- Uranus spotting --
Early observations -- Uranus in the solar system -- Uranus and Earth --
Missions to Uranus -- Uranus explorer: William Herschel -- Uranus
explorer: Leslye Boyce -- Uranus on the web -- Activity: Uranus math --
What have you learned?
  ISBN 1-59036-097-4 (lib. bdg. : alk. paper) – ISBN 1-59036-224-1 (pbk.)
  1. Uranus (Planet)--Juvenile literature. [1. Uranus (Planet)] I.
Title. II. Series.
  QB681 .R56 2003
  523.47--dc21
                              2002014501

Printed in the United States of America
1 2 3 4 5 6 7 8 9 0 08 07 06 05 04

Photograph Credits

Every reasonable effort has been made to trace ownership and to obtain permission to reprint
copyright material. The publishers would be pleased to have any errors or omissions brought
to their attention so that they may be corrected in subsequent printings.

Cover: Tom Stack & Associates (top); Digital Vision (bottom)

Virginia Boulay: pages 8, 12; **COMSTOCK, Inc.:** page 11; **CORBIS/MAGMA:** pages 6 (Bettmann), 18
(Bettmann), 22 (Christel Gerstenberg); **Digital Stock Corporation:** page 21; **Digital Vision:** page 14;
NASA: pages 13, 16, 17, 19; **Tom Stack & Associates:** pages 4 (NASA/JPL), 7 (TSADO/NASA), 9
(TSADO/NASA); **Visuals Unlimited:** pages 1, 10.

Project Coordinator Jennifer Nault **Design** Terry Paulhus
Substantive Editor Heather Kissock **Copy Editor** Tina Schwartzenberger
Layout Virginia Boulay and Bryan Pezzi **Photo Researcher** Tina Schwartzenberger

Contents

Introducing Uranus

Uranus has been in the sky for billions of years. It was only discovered about 200 years ago. This giant planet is puzzling in many ways. It glows blue-green in the night sky. Its **orbit** is also very unusual. Uranus is an interesting planet. Read on to find out more about the seventh planet from the Sun.

The gas that surrounds Uranus gives it a blue-green glow.

Uranus Facts

- Most often, a planet stands upright on its **axis**. Uranus is different. It is tilted on its side.

- For many years, **astronomers** believed that Uranus was a star.

- Uranus is the third largest planet after Jupiter and Saturn.

- Uranus has a **core** made of rock. This core is surrounded by a deep sea.

- The planet's **atmosphere** is made of several gases, mostly hydrogen and helium.

- Uranus is one of the four planets called gas giants. The other three are Jupiter, Saturn, and Neptune.

Name That Planet

Uranus was named for the Greek god Ouranos. Ancient Greeks believed that Ouranos was the god of the sky. This god is also one of the first gods in Greek **mythology**. His wife is Gaea, the goddess of the Earth. Ouranos is the grandfather of Zeus, the ruler of all the gods. In Roman mythology, Zeus is known as Jupiter.

Ouranos's son Cronus was known as Saturn in Roman mythology.

Uranus's Moons

Astronomers discovered four new moons around Uranus in 1999. The planet has twenty-one known moons. Uranus's largest moons are made of ice and rock. Many of the surface features of these moons were formed by ice melting and freezing. This action caused the surface to crack.

Titania is the name given to Uranus's largest moon. Cordelia is the tiniest of Uranus's moons.

■ Titania is Uranus's largest moon, but it is smaller than Earth's moon.

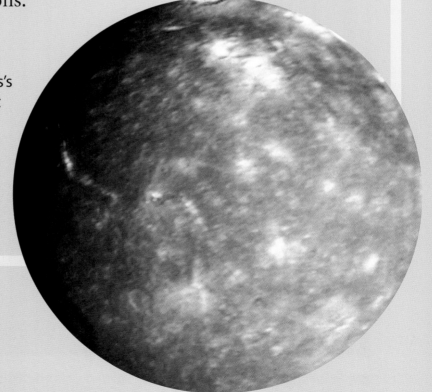

Uranus Spotting

In 1977, astronomers saw something strange happen to Uranus. It all began when the planet passed in front of a star. Uranus's light began to fade, then shine again. The planet appeared to be winking. This unusual activity led to an important discovery. Astronomers realized that Uranus had rings around it.

■ Scientists once believed that Saturn was the only planet with rings. They were surprised when they discovered Uranus's rings.

Uranus's Rings

There are eleven known rings around Uranus. They are made of ice boulders and dust. The rings around Uranus are very dark in color. They are some of the darkest objects in our **solar system**.

Scientists have discovered smaller rings within each of Uranus's rings. These are called ringlets.

■ The rings of Uranus look like straight lines in a photograph. This is because the ring pieces move very quickly in space. They move too quickly to take a still image.

Early Observations

For years, people thought that Saturn was the last planet in our solar system. Uranus was finally discovered on March 13, 1781.

Uranus is very far away from Earth. This means that it is difficult to see in the night sky. People once thought that the planet was just a dim star. In 1690, an astronomer named John Flamsteed observed Uranus in the sky. He believed that the planet was a star.

■ John Flamsteed named Uranus "34 Tauri." This name identified Uranus as a star.

See for Yourself

Uranus is not an easy planet to spot in the evening sky. Many early star watchers did not even notice it. Only on very clear nights can Uranus be seen without binoculars or a **telescope**.

You need to know where to look for Uranus to find it in the sky. Ask science center staff to help you locate Uranus. Try using a pair of binoculars if there is no telescope available.

■ Uranus looks like a faint blue-green disk in the sky when it is viewed through a telescope.

Uranus in Our Solar System

Uranus is one of the nine planets in our solar system. It is the seventh planet from the Sun.

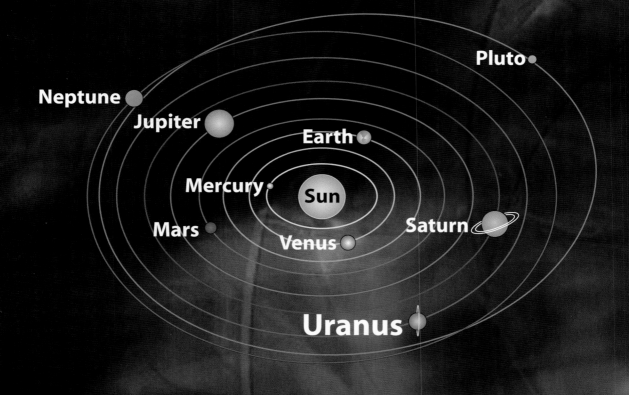

Pluto

Neptune

Jupiter

Earth

Mercury

Sun

Mars

Saturn

Venus

Uranus

Liquid makes up most of Uranus's total volume.

Uranus's atmosphere extends about 3,100 miles (4,989 kilometers) above the planet.

Uranus and Earth

All nine planets in our solar system orbit the Sun. It takes about 365 days for Earth to complete an orbit. This is the length of Earth's year. Uranus is much farther from the Sun than Earth is. It takes Uranus much longer to complete an orbit because it has farther to travel. It takes about 84 Earth years to make 1 year on Uranus.

■ Earth is nineteen times closer to the Sun than Uranus is. This is why temperatures on Earth are much warmer.

Compare the Planets

PLANET FEATURES					
PLANET	**Distance from the Sun**	**Days to Orbit the Sun**	**Diameter**	**Length of Day**	**Average Temperature**
Mercury	36 million miles (58 million km)	88	3,032 miles (4,880 km)	4,223 hours	333° Fahrenheit (167° C)
Venus	67 million miles (108 million km)	225	7,521 miles (12,104 km)	2,802 hours	867° Fahrenheit (464° C)
Earth	93 million miles (150 million km)	365	7,926 miles (12,756 km)	24 hours	59° Fahrenheit (15° C)
Mars	142 million miles (229 million km)	687	4,222 miles (6,975 km)	25 hours	−81° Fahrenheit (−63° C)
Jupiter	484 million miles (779 million km)	4,331	88,846 miles (142,984 km)	10 hours	−230° Fahrenheit (−146° C)
Saturn	891 million miles (1,434 million km)	10,747	74,897 miles (120,535 km)	11 hours	−285° Fahrenheit (−176° C)
Uranus	1,785 million miles (2,873 million km)	30,589	31,763 miles (51,118 km)	17 hours	−355° Fahrenheit (−215° C)
Neptune	2,793 million miles (4,495 million km)	59,800	30,775 miles (49,528 km)	16 hours	−355° Fahrenheit (−215° C)
Pluto	3,647 million miles (5,869 million km)	90,588	1,485 miles (2,390 km)	153 hours	−375° Fahrenheit (−226° C)

Missions to Uranus

Voyager 2 is a **space probe**. It has given us most of the information we have about Uranus. The probe was launched in 1977. First, it passed Jupiter and Saturn. It reached Uranus after 9 years of travel. It snapped photographs of its moons and rings. Because of this mission, ten new moons were found.

Later, NASA's *Hubble Space Telescope* took pictures of Uranus. These pictures showed that powerful storms sometimes occur on Uranus. Most storms happen in the spring.

■ *Voyager 2* took 7,000 photographs of Uranus.

Cloudy Weather

Uranus has mild weather compared to Jupiter and Saturn. Still, wispy clouds have been sighted above the planet. These clouds move in the same direction that Uranus spins on its axis. Blowing winds make these clouds move at fast speeds. Uranus's clouds form into long bands.

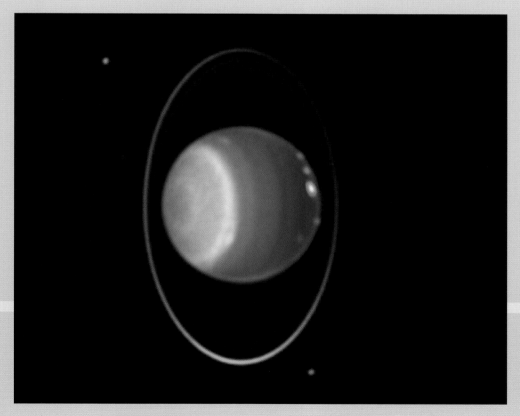

The *Hubble Space Telescope* discovered long bands of clouds on Uranus in 1998.

William Herschel

Name: William Herschel
Uranus Accomplishments: Identified Uranus as a planet

Uranus was first identified as a planet in 1781. A man named William Herschel made the discovery. William worked as a music teacher in England. In his spare time, he built telescopes and studied the stars. He discovered the planet by accident, while he was studying stars.

William's discovery made him famous. He quickly became the head astronomer for the king of England. William wanted to name the planet after the king. It was named after the Greek god Ouranos instead.

■ William spotted Uranus with a telescope that he built himself.

Leslye Boyce

Name: Leslye Boyce
Uranus Accomplishments:
Repairs the *Hubble Space Telescope* flight computers

Leslye Boyce works for NASA. She keeps the flight computers for the *Hubble Space Telescope* in working order. This telescope has taken photographs of Uranus. Leslye plans and watches over new computer programs. For instance, she helped to set up a new flight computer on the *Hubble Space Telescope* in 1999. Computers that are used in space have to be strong. They are often made out of special materials.

The *Hubble Space Telescope* has taken many photographs of Uranus. These images are helping scientists learn more about the planet.

Uranus on the Internet

To learn more about Uranus, look for books at your school library. The Internet is also an excellent place to learn about Uranus. There are many great Web sites with information. Just type the words *Uranus* and *planet* into a search engine. Google and Yahoo are useful search engines.

The Internet has information on all of the planets in our solar system. To learn about the nine planets, visit these Web sites:

Encarta Homepage
www.encarta.com
Type the name of a planet that you would like to learn about into the search engine.

NASA Kids
http://kids.msfc.nasa.gov
NASA built a Web site for young learners just like you. Visit this site to learn more about the nine planets, space travel, and the latest NASA news.

Young Scientists at Work

Uranus **rotates** on its side. This experiment will show you how Uranus spins in space.

You will need:

- a piece of strong string, such as twine

- a long, thick needle with a large eye

- a very small orange

Cut a piece of string the length of your arm. Thread the string through the needle. Tie a knot around the eye of the needle with one end of the string. Carefully poke the needle through the orange. Be sure to push the needle out through the other side of the fruit. Slowly pull the string through the orange until it is the same length on both sides. Remove the needle from the end of the string.

Grasp onto each end of the string. Hold the orange and string away from your body. Now, begin spinning the fruit by moving both ends of the string in little circles. The motion of the orange is similar to Uranus's rotation.

What Have You Learned?

How much do you know about Uranus?
Test your knowledge!

1 What is unusual about the way Uranus spins on its axis?

2 What color is Uranus?

3 Who observed Uranus through a homemade telescope?

4 Name the space probe that gave scientists information about Uranus.

5 How many moons does Uranus have?

6 What is the name of the telescope that has taken many photographs of Uranus?

7 True or False?
There is ice on
Uranus's moons.

8 Which planet is larger,
Earth or Uranus?

9 Are the rings around
Uranus dark or light
in color?

10 How long is one year
on Uranus?

What was your score?

9–10	You should work at NASA!
5–8	Not too bad for an earthling!
0–4	You need to polish your telescope!

Answers

1 Uranus is tilted on its side as it spins on its axis. **2** Uranus glows a blue-green color.
3 William Herschel **4** *Voyager 2* **5** Uranus has twenty-one moons. **6** The *Hubble Space Telescope* **7** True. Uranus has several moons with ice on their surface. **8** Uranus is larger. It is four times bigger than Earth. **9** The rings around Uranus are the darkest objects in space. **10** A year on Uranus is equal to 84 Earth years.

Words to Know

astronomers: people who study space and its objects

atmosphere: the layer of gases surrounding a planet

axis: an imaginary line on which a planet spins

core: the central part of a planet

mythology: stories or legends, often about gods or heroes

orbit: the nearly circular path a space object makes around another object in space

rotates: spinning motion

solar system: the Sun, the planets, and other objects that move around the Sun

space probe: a spacecraft used to gather information about space

telescope: an instrument that uses lenses to make distant objects appear closer

Index